Hello kookaburra!

and other Australian birds

by Natalie Jane Parker and Luisa Adam

BROLLY books

eastern rosellas

pee-p-twee
pee-p-twee
pee-p-twee

We are **eastern rosellas**.

We have colourful feathers of **red**, **blue**, **green**, **yellow**, and **white**.

We like to sing songs, and we whistle a sweet tweeting tune.

Our friends in the trees hop about and make a 'beep-peep' sound.

Can you guess who they are?

beep-pee-p!

beep-pee-p!

beep-pee-p!

We are **zebra finches**.

Our feathers are **grey** and **white** with patches of **brown** and **black**.

Our beaks are bright **orange**.

We have **black** 'teardrop' marks below our eyes. Sometimes we have dark stripes around our throats.

We can see our friends fishing by the river. They make an 'ee-ee' sound.

Do you know who they are?

zebra finches

azure kingfishers

ee!ee!
ee!ee!
ee!ee!
ee!ee!

We are **azure kingfishers**.

We have **blue** feathers with an **orange** belly and a **white** throat. Our tail is short and **blue**.

We use our long, sharp beaks to catch the fish we love to eat.

Nearby are some noisy black birds. They call out to each other in screeches.

Do you know who they are?

screech!

screech!

We are **black cockatoos**.

We are large, noisy birds. Our feathers are mostly **black**.

Some of us have **yellow** marks on our cheeks and tails.

We like to fly high in the sky, calling loudly to each other.

Down below, we can hear some little birds. They are singing a song with a trill.

Do you know who they are?

black cockatoos

fairy wrens

t-rrrl-l-l-lllllllllll

t-rrrl-l-l-lllllllllll

We are **fairy wrens**.

We are small and dainty. We come in many shades of **white** and **blue** and **brown** and **grey**.

Our bodies are round and our wings are short. Our tails often stand up behind us.

In the trees above is a noisy and colourful bird. Sometimes we can hear him screeching to his friends.

Do you know who he is?

screeee-arch!

screeee-arch!

I am a **rainbow lorikeet**.

My beak is bright **red**, my head is **blue**, my wings are **green**, and my chest is **yellow** and **orange**.

I perch in trees or fly high in the sky.

I can hear a 'boom' in the distance. It sounds just like a drum.

Do you know who is making that noise?

rainbow lorikeet

boom!
boom!
boom!
boom!

I am an **emu**, the biggest bird in Australia!

I have a long neck and a sharp beak. My feathers are **brown** with **white** patches and **black** tips. My neck is **blue**.

Near the sea, I have friends who chatter a lot and make a 'gaw gaw' sound. They have flippers instead of wings!

Can you guess who they are?

emu

fairy penguins

gaw! gaw-gaw!

gaw-gaw!

gaw! gaw!

We are **fairy penguins**, the smallest in our family.

We have dark **blue** feathers on our backs and heads, and our bellies are **white**.

We use our flippers to swim, and we do not fly.

Our beaks are long and pointed. Our feet are webbed, like a duck's.

Nearby, a family of colourful birds are whistling a song.

Do you know who they are?

tweet!
tweet!
tweet!
tweet!

tweet! tweet!
tweet! tweet!
tweet!
tweet! tweet!
tweet!
tweet!

We are **king parrots**.

Our backs are **green** and our bellies are **red**. The feathers on our heads are **red** for boys and **green** for girls. We have some **blue** feathers, too.

We all have long tails and curved beaks.

Some noisy, laughing birds live near us.

Do you know who they are?

hoo-hoo-hoo!

ha-ha-ha!

We are **kookaburras**.

Our heads and bellies are **white** and our backs and wings are **brown**. We have a **brown** band of feathers around our eyes. Our wings are often tipped with **blue**.

Sometimes we snuggle up together along a branch.

We can hear an 'ark! ark!' sound close by.

Do you know who is making that noise?

ha-ha-ha!

pink cockatoos

ark! ark!
ark! ark!
ark!

We are **pink cockatoos**.

We have pale **pink** feathers and **white** wings.

The crests on our heads are **white** and open up to show colours of **red** and **yellow**.

We spend a lot of time eating and looking for food.

We can see a black-and-white bird below. He is making a warbling sound.

Do you know who he is?

m
a
g
p
i
e

agh!

I am a **magpie**.
My feathers are **black**
and **white**. My beak
is **white** with a
black tip.

Here I am, drinking
from a tap.

I am very clever and
often very cheeky!